Verb Sap

Creative Commons Attribution-Noncommercial-Share Alike 3.0 License.

Parts of this book may be reproduced & appropriated with permission from the author for noncommercial purposes only.

Printed in the United States of America.
2008

ISBN 10: 0-9793901-1-7
ISBN 13: 978-0-9793901-1-1
Library of Congress Number: 9780979390111

narrow house
4523 Mainfield Ave
Baltimore, Maryland 21214

narrowhouse.org

First Edition

2 4 6 8 0 9 7 5 3 1

Backtracking (Upon Dylan Thomas), *Oar Through*, and *Riff* appear in the Schizotype issue of WORD at Peekreview.net, then in the loose leaf edition of WORD's Schizotype.

My Silent Confidante and *Vermifuge* appear in SUCCESS! - Chimera: I Am My Own Twin.

Intromit appeared in Shattered Wig #27.

for Manya, Hero, and Gryphon

Contents

Anthem	9
Backtracking (Upon Dylan Thomas)	10
Carnage or Afterimage	11
Riff	13
My Silent Confidant	16
Oar Through	17
This	19
Radical Crumb	21
Empirical / Imperial Demonstration	23
Verb Sap	24
Backtracking Prufrock	33
Intromit	40
Lust We Be Misunderstood	42
Stay Free	47
Brecht in Santa Monica (1941-1947)	56
Marcuse at UCSD (1965-1970)	57
Antaeus / Anchises	58
Birdman in a No-Fly Zone	59
Thole Econometrica, Thole Apocalypse	63
Vermifuge	67
Anthem / Anathema	69

Anthem

Backtracking (Upon Dylan Thomas)

In my cradle or sulky arson
Exempted in the stiletto of niggard
When only the mood rags
And the lovebirds lick abeam
With all their gridirons in their arks,
I label by sinning ligature
Not for ambiance or breach
Or the strumpet and tractor of charlatans
On the ivied stags
But for the commodious wags
Of their most second-string hearse.

Not for the protean mammoth apace
From the ragging mood I wrinkle
On these spindle pagans
Nor for the tough-minded day-to-day
With their nighties and prunes
But for the lovebirds, their arks
Round the gridirons of the agaves,
Who pawn no prairie or wags
Nor hedgehop my cradle or arson.

Carnage or Afterimage

Torquemada the motorcycle brings you over the
    edge
cliff climax
inquisition into adsorptive surfaces
materials science
sibylline, the Delphic tripod, the oracle
in triplicate
Ponder.
activated charcoal attracts toxic gas molecules
viruses adsorb too to cells, similarly
microbes aerobic or an-
breathe fresh air
there's the rub, gas masks advertising vapors
ads' orb and rupture   zorbing
you zorbing
carnage or afterimage bimetallic not bent not pinion
film formation
the surface of a solid   or liquid
that sibyl not only sonogram
how many grams to get you pinning
rapture, an interruption   iron
steel, trot, dial it, and dilate
coke and charcoal irruption, inanition
rapture, rupture, irruption interrupts
pinned pinions   Pegasi
when she triplicates her cliff and self, duplicitously
three-legged race, Red-Handed Jill, sighs
and the racist island.   and then the racist island.
Jilling.
adsorb the asocial and vanguard or baroque

to Zorba the Buddha from Osho aka Rajneesh
accumulation of gasses, liquids, and solutes
in opinion
not bent
Ponder.
ripple gates and the pearl on the tongue curvaceous
it's on the tip of the tongue, adsorption
and the absurd curdled
noxiousness for symptomatic interalia
sacked

Prologue
     In which we learn that Jimmy Corrigan, the smartest kid on Earth, is a lonely emotionally-impaired Human Castaway.
     "I am a lonely emotionally-impaired Human Castaway," it says in a speech bubble next to the silhouette of a small house, light from narrow windows rendered a lighter peach within the panel's two-tone color of black and dull peach.

in the sack
are you calling it a sex cult, or sects or phone cult
a charismatic
a colt, clit
occult guilt
also adsorptive of reddish jillions in steed
instead of retinal negatives and upside feedback
upside-down visuals to draw a bead on
the rational
stunning further
zoom-zoom, a guru
in after words
Ponder.

Riff

Either the single individual can stand
The single individual can stand in
Individual as the single
An absolute relation to the absolute

Either the single
In an absolute relation
As the single
The absolute
Consequently

Is not the highest

Is not the highest
The absolute, and
The ethical
Either
Or Abraham is lost

Abraham is lost

Abraham is lost
And consequently
Either a relation to the absolute
Is not the highest
An absolute relation
The single individual as the single individual

An absolute relation
Absolute, and

Highest, or

The ethical
Either

Single and consequently
Can stand

The individual
Can stand in

The absolute

In an absolute relation to the absolute
The single as the single
And consequently the highest

The ethical is not the highest
Consequently
Abraham is

Abraham is
Either the single individual
Or

An absolute relation to the absolute

As the single individual can stand in
The single individual
Consequently an absolute relation
And the ethical is not the highest
The absolute

Either the single individual can stand

The single individual can stand in
An absolute
Individual stand in
Relation to the absolute

Either the single individual can stand the single individual
In absolute relation to the absolute

Or Abraham is lost

Or Abraham is lost

Or Abraham is lost

My Silent Confidant

The one kind and the other. Syntax, and sin tax. Shot, to replace should. In pursuance of ligatures. Many grave calculus on the calling. I uncharitably thought. Either the single individual as the single individual or. Quoting Kierkegaard. When we got fairly on the road, I haunt laughed, I haunt echoed.

Riffs, and sniff test. Miser and misery. Empire, for the intangible. Unless it is to confirm what. Cloud nine lowering on it, the reverence. Who was so officious to help. Repetition, whether or not it is possible. K's *Repetition*. When we got fairly on the road was to appear as old as possible to the coachman.

How I shot proceed, ignition. Inanition, and the inane. We're both adulterers, aren't we? I mean adults. Proposal so very ungraciously. A tawdry Leila. Dumplings uncommon fine down there. Whether or not it is possible, echo. The ethical is not the highest. I alternate hungry, horny, happy, hurt.

The single individual and the ethical. Absolute, and highest. Imperial empirical. Stymied, on that he vent. Not dossier, but making a hash of it. Cloud lowering, whatever wile bay wile bay. Constantin Constantius is K. Behind a low wingbacked partition. "My love cannot find expression in a marriage." Come again? The others who disown you. The others you disown.

Shouldn't, or haunted. Constancy. That operation of kissing the sticks of her fan. Forgive me for addressing you so familiarly. Singled inhale and mincemeat. Repetition, that operation of kissing the sticks. Hey, Baby, k-k-k-k-k-k, if you're single, let's suspend the ethical, absolutely. Sniff test the sty mead. It's a golf term, and has to do with not seeing obstructions, orig. Actually, that might be better if you're married.

Oar Through

the whole, the hole, soul-thole
awl and trawling, oar through
all through
work a bit of leather

work over
hell for letters
or through
the ole finicky

finitude

albeit
I'll bite
I'll buy it
that's fine

Braille-reading the lake for angling
checking out the angles
for an invitation to the next

maiming

another kind of wanting something
dip a moody hand in it

that's fine, by a hair
fur angling
laces
eyelet

lashes

a slave

a love-slave for drowning
in another's eye-dilation

access denied

it's alive
it's a wake

it's still asking for it

This

Don't read this this way, and hear this this way, hear it my way. Hear it your way my way, but hear it that way in reading it, hear it in your head, and if I'm reading it, hear it that way, listen. I'm reading it in writing it anyways. And then I'll read it. This. Please read this and hear this the way I mean it, listen to me in how I am saying this. Or don't listen to me, but hear this. This. As Heraclitus meant and said, "Listen not to me, but to the *Logos*." What did that mean? That. That that. *Logos* translated as The Word, or the words, or the account. Don't read it that way, but this way; don't hear it that way, but this way. Heraclitus' way; or your way Heraclitus' way. *Logos* is neither The Word nor the words. It isn't don't listen to me, listen to my words—no, don't listen to my words, listen to my mouth—no! Is it? This. Don't listen to me, listen to the *Logos*, and I'll have to say it with *Kairos*, to be heard. To be understood. Not the words, and it doesn't do to allow any particular word to be propped up as The Word. To be heard, I'll have to say it with *Kairos*; to be heard in what I mean, I must say what I mean in context, in Time, according to the times, in this. Within the given framework for understanding, understand? Within the given culture, within the given language, within the given style, within the given form, within the given context, with the given contents. These are the contents for you to know what I mean, know what I mean? These. In this. In this temporality. Reading it this way, hearing it this way. *Kairos*. Hearing this this way, in the timing. This, this time. This, this timing. And again, this. Then again, this. Then again there's the animated version of *The Last Unicorn*, a seventies movie—no, it's about the times again, the timing, it was actually made in the early eighties when many things still felt like the seventies. The movie *The Last Unicorn*, with soundtrack by America, in which a roving butterfly, a hep beret-wearing butterfly, a non-answerer, an evasive flutterer—and sunny sometime flatterer—seems to be quoting Heraclitus, "No, no, listen! Don't listen to me, listen!" Suddenly, for that moment of truth, *Kairos* in the flitting of wing-thin songs and phrases, amidst incessant overturnings, "Listen! Listen, listen quickly!" This, quickly. And this, and this, and this. Then this, and this, and this. This particular this. This part, this. And as a whole, this. This whole this. This, in this moment. And that, that moment. That passed moment, that past moment. This, in that. That, in this. Read this that way, hear this that way. This way. All of this. Listen.

Radical Crumb

Testing the crumb. Tasting the crumb. Choosing fork or fingers. Following the recipe or improvising. Substituting ingredients. Testing it for you. Taking a bite of yours. Deciding upon coffee cake, buttercrumb, or the traditional crumbcake. Is this related to streusel, or other cross-genres? If, and how much, when it comes to confectioners' sugar. Picking off the crumbs. Poking a finger into the cake. Reading My Troubles with Women, by R. Crumb. Carefully separating the crumb from the tin. Are the bigger ones really better? One has to scoop the little ones in the cradle of one's fork. Even when full, forging onwards into the crumbs. Forgoing the crumbs. Getting tired of the same old thing week after week. Giving up on ever finding the perfect crumb, or a truly original crumb, or even a recipe whose basic approach hasn't been tried before. Settling for the usual crumb. Or giving up on ever finding again the first crumb loved so well, the inspiring crumb, the crumb that inspired all this, the Muse-crumb. Or ever regaining that sensation or emotion or deep-seated feeling or state of first experiencing it with a novice's relish. With a learner's relish—that virgin relish. The revelation of crumb. Nostalgia for crumb. Hope for crumb. A hamster on the wheel for crumb. The vanity of mortal wishes. But something keeps you going. The eternal crumbling drives you on. Faith in achieving something through the crumb. Acceptance of possible folly, of a fated false path. The calling of crumb. The crumby but defensible song, "Someone left the cake out in the rain." You're out of crumb, after I traveled half the world and faced countless preposterous dangers? I'll have the Siberian peach pie. But next week I'll search for crumb again, no joke. Wallowing in the crumbiness as a spiritual discipline. It's the end of a long story. Celebrating the crumb. Sometimes it's more crumb than cake, but arguably that's the best part. Relatively speaking, certainly it's the best part to some. Every crumb is a microcosm, but not every crumb is equal. People deny it, but there's an absolute value to the crumb, and maybe that's not even what it should be called. Maybe "crumb" doesn't do it justice. Perhaps we are denigrating ourselves, when we don't need to. Say it, eat it. To deny it is to deny ourselves perhaps. There's justification in the crumb, vindication for the world. I never really gave up on it. Reading of crumb on the box: "The Ultimate Crumbcake." One has to have aspirations.

Empirical / Imperial Demonstration

The difference between
    what is seen   and what is not seen
        what is heard   and unheard
            what is touched   and intangible

isn't the difference between
    what is there   and

Verb Sap

Verbsap,

yet we keep on
babbling

and call that our
Art Thou
sufficient unto your
                shelf

a word to the
why I've

never been able to fathom
the foam on the beach

seablast

but the kids are digging
to China
and who's to disabuse
                them?

Certainly not the
adulterated cankers

on the jellyfish
washed ashore.

Isn't that what they call

                        soughing,
there in the shallows?

How neap.

What a tidy
set of teeth
you've got chattering
across the table

did you wind it up
for chuckles half past
the nightly showdown?

Where's the key?

A laminate the color of sand.

Someone hit the dirt at
Hi no one.

Faced first
the emptiness of
howling

winds, tumbleweeds,
swinging saloon doors

sixshooter tropes
popping caps

and I can't tell you
how many times
we've seen

the making of.

Yet this is the vanguard,
'tis pity.

Want a tip?
Fourteen percent

is no longer enough
to live on

landfill subdivisions

but who's to ask anyone
to give it their

All Clear
bulldozers at the ready

snakepit cocktails at the party
wall

don't bother knocking
unless you know the code

* * *

It's more than that, though.
Stop me before

I could go on

perchance, should we

learn the word "aleatory"?

Define die.

I'm not trying to be cruel,
but I'm not moved

and I'm not moving.

I like it here, with
the trowels

and slick interstices
of mortal
remains

of the daybed refutation.

You've already made yourself
comfortable
that's obviated

any need for anything special?

Put it out of your mind.

                      ***

It's too easy

like hating and making fun of
the POTUS

and other public fingers

pointing

out how you're into

animalia, the web-footed
genus

in place of acculturated
ingenuity of soar throat
comfits

new flavors, it's an industry.

Lapidary reds, purples,
yellow-golds as translucent
as syrup

see through

night crawlers, nightshade,
night soil

but there's something alive and
shining in the mud!—

maggots.

Forgive them their
sincerest

waiting for a
form of

apostasy

imago that, and
eidolons this

forgive them their waiting
for a metamorphosis

while we stroll along eidolons
                                            road,

idly happy.

Oddly, it's a fly

and someone I have the
utmost respect for
is an anti-fly fanatic.

Me? I'll try anything,
Once.

                    ***

First scribbled this
in a tiny notebook

labeled "The Courtly Art
of the Ancient Maya."

Coincidence? Week
of the opening

of the National Museum of
the American Indian

and we're strong again

in "each their own way"

bound with a strip of red tape
and an orange paper cover.

Polemical and totemic
for becoming a center
through decentering

rightly so, left
to one's own

devices
of liberation, free

domain

Codex Tlingit

looks like I'll be spending
a lot of time there
finishing up

a fourteen-year
Raven tattoo
appropriation

for my own purposes.

Sing it!

* * *

Sorry, this is getting personal
please don't tip my canoe

it's icy out there
so I row from island
                    to island

at least I've painted eyes
in black formlines on the
                    prow
red glints

it doesn't hurt when I
crunch into the snowbank

sorry, again,
but I'm not impressed
by the available housing

and that affects one's welcome

                  * * *

How come I have to love you
so damn much?

And I do, though

I do.

God bleed it all over my knife.

What did they actually do,

at the top of the pyramid,
during a human sacrifice?

That was Cortez' excuse.

Yet, in spite of it all,
I continue to find
ship-burning stratagems
useful.

                * * *

So who's the better fighter?

If there were a tactful
means of examining
bruises

it would still only be in a
subcutaneous context.

Where's the cut?
The deeper

execution
of endgame affirmations.

Are we getting to yes yet?

Backtracking Prufrock

Lessen us gnaw then, you and I
When the eve is sprayed out against the skunk
Like a patience etched upon a tabernacle;
Lessen us gnaw, through ceremonious halfcocked
    streamliners,
The mutilating retorts
Of restive niggards in one-horse chatty hotboxes
And saw rests with oxtails:
Streamliners that fold like a technical argot
Of inshore intensity
To leach you to an overweening quest…
Oh, divulge not ascribe, "What irrupts it?"
Lessen us gnaw and maintain our vision.

In the rookery the wombats combine and gnaw
Taking of Methuselah.

The yeasty foe that rows its bacillus upon the
    window-dressing,
The yeasty smog that rows its muumuu on the
    window-dressing,
Liberated its tongs into the corneas of the eve,
Lined upon the poodles that stampede in dragoons,
Lessened fake upon its bacillus the sonnet that fakes
    from chimeras,
Slunk by the tern, maddened a suchlike lean-to,
And seducing that it warranted a sodden Oceania
    niggard,
Cured oftentimes aborning the houri, and felicitated
    aslant.

And incommunicado there wile bay timbre
For the yeasty smog that slices along the
	streamliners
Rowing its bacillus upon the window-dressing;
There wile bay timbre, there wile bay timbre
To prepackage a façade to meditate the façades that
	you meditate;
There wile bay timbre to munch and crease,
And timbre for alkaline the wordings and dawns
That lie and droop a quest on your plasterboard;
Timbre for you and timbre for me,
And timbre yes for a hunchback incudes,
And for a hunchback visibilities and reversals,
Before the takeover of a toady and T-bone.

In the rookery the wombats combine and gnaw
Taking of Methuselah.

And incommunicado there wile bay timbre
To wolf, "Divulge I dapple?" and "Divulge I
	dapple?"
Timbre to tumble babyishly and descant the stain,
With a baggy sportswriter in the midden of my
	hailstorm—
(They wile saw: "How his hailstorm is groveling
	thick-skinned!")
My morn coastline, my collage mottling finitely to
	the chimpanzee,
My neckline ribald and modern, but assembled by a
	simpatico pimple—
(They wile saw: "But how his arks and leftovers
	arch thick-skinned!")
Divulge I dapple

Distribute the univalve?
In a minuet there irrupts timbre
For decimeters and reversals which a minuet wile revere.

For I haunt knocked them all aloud, knocked them all—
Haunt knocked the eves, morns, aftermaths,
I haunt meandered otherwise my lieutenant with coelenterate spools;
I knock the vogues dyeing with a dyeing fake
Below the mushroom from a far-sighted rookery.
    So how shot I pressurize?

And I haunt knocked the exurbias aloud, knocked them all—
The exurbias that fit you in a formalized photosynthesis,
And when I am formalized, spouting on a pimple,
When I am pimped and wrestling on the walkup,
Then how shot I beget
To spirit otherwise alkaline the buttes of my dawns and waxworks?
    And how shot I pressurize?

And I haunt knocked the arks aloud, knocked them all—
Arks that are braced and whimsical and barbarous
(But in the lampblack, downcast with lifelong broody hailstorm!)
Irrupts it performance from a dredge
That maintains me snidely digest?
Arks that lick aloft a tabernacle, or wrangle about a shaver.

And shot I then pressurize?
And how shot I beget?

***

Shot I saw, I haunt golfed at duress through
    nameless streamliners
And wasted the smog that ripples from the pips
Of lone memories in shirting, leaking out of
    windmills?...

I shot haunt beefed a painting of raffish claviers
Scurrying across the floodlights of significant
    scythes.

***

And the aftermath, the eve, sleeks snidely
    patronizingly!
Smoked by lonesome finesses,
Aslant…tipsy…or it maligns,
Stressed on the floodlight, here beside you and me.
Shot I, after T-bone and caissons and ibises,
Haunt the streetwalker to forbid the mollycoddle to
    his cripple?
But though I haunt went and fashioned, went and
    prattled,
Though I haunt seemed my H-bomb (growled
    slickly baggy)
brooked impurely upon a platoon,
I alternate no prophecy—and here's no gray matte;
I haunt seemed the mollycoddle of my greatcoat
    flick,
And I haunt seemed the estimable Footlocker hoist

    my coastline,
        and sneeze,
And in short, I warranted aforethought.
And worst it haunt beefed worth it, after all,
After the cumuli, the marlingspike, the T-bone,
Among the populism, among somber talisman of
    you and me,
Worst it haunt beefed worthless,
To haunt bitched o'er the matte with a smilax,
To haunt squealed the univalve into a balk
To roil it toward somber overweening quest,
To saw: "I alternate Lafayette, combine from the
    day-to-day,
Combine babyishly to televise you all, I shake
    televise you all"—
If one, setting a pillory by her H-bomb,
Shot saw: "That irrupts not what I might at
    all.
        That irrupts not it, at all."

And worst it haunt beefed worth it, after all,
Worst it haunt beefed worthless,
After the sunroofs and the doorways and the sprung
    streamliners,
After the novas, after the teachings, after the
    skirmishes that
traffic along the floodlight—
And this, and snidely mostly mordancy?—
It irrupts imposing to saw judiciously what I might!
But as if a magenta lantana threshed the nepotisms
    in patters on a screech:
Worst it haunt beefed worthless
If one, setting a pillory or throttling o'er a shaver,
And tunneling toward the windmill, shot saw:

"That irrupts not it at all.
That irrupts not what I might, at all."

***

No! I alternate not Mister Hamilton, nor warranted
    maximized to bay;
Alternate an attendance loot, one that wile divulge
To sweeten a programming, stare a scenario or two,
Advertise the mister; no doubloon, an eastern
    tonsure,
Defensive, glacial to bay of usage,
Polite, caustic, and meteoric;
Frumpy of hideous sensor, but a bistro
    obstreperous;
At timbres, incommunicado, all told rickety—
All told, at timbres, the Foodstuff.

I grovel oily…I grovel oily…
I shake wean the bottleneck of my troupers roiled.

Shake I parse my hailstorm beforehand? Divulge I
    dapple ease a peacetime?
I shake wean whimsical flank troupers, and waken
    upon the bazooka.
I haunt heaped the meritocracies sinning, each to
    each.

I divulge not thieve that they wile sin to me.

I haunt seemed them riddling seasonably on the
    wattles.
Color-coding the whimsical hailstorm of the wattles
    bloused babyish

When the winch blouses the watchword whimsical
   and bizarre.

We haunt lined in the challises of the scythe
By seafood wreaked with seaway recumbent and
   brotherly
Till hulking vogues waive us and we drop.

Intromit

intromit

the stucco of interior slatherings
casings
pop-pop-pop
the holeable in perception
the o of the mouth
nowhere is it more applicable
involute
than in volumes outside the range of hearing
then in volumes strange and left-handed
and warping out the shape of your gastrula

a reverb
faced with bends sinister
the bends
otherwise know as caisson disease
the caissons fit for topology
bridging the gaps
it's watertight but not about Earth
star-stretching, or just getting to the surface
from under reaching towards the sun splashed
    across
where the bubbles rise to and nitrogen
pop

the surface of the water
not calm
but breathing wavily

a liquid topography for maps
to what treasure
to what knowing
ripples instead of guidelines
instead of indications
o's.

with a trickle of brown-glopped blood on the seared
    rim,
oozy.

entry point or sphincter
it certainly quivers to the touch, to the probing
of a digit, of a character, of a mark.

resigned to be multi-symptomatic
it's glaring
its glaring
the Uzi, the shadows, the blinding shock
and humdrum surprising details
(finding out you *can* have it both ways)
fabulous insinuate and disassembled
semblances

of flesh, of fullness, of filled space—
yet there isn't release in the slit.

a bit of dried blood for solace, the sealed rim.

Lust We Be Misunderstood

this is rocket science
not plumbing

in search of ghost leaks
process of elimination

when the pipes are under the slab
and you'll have to take a jackhammer
to the kitchen floor

tiles
that's crossing the line
isolating the problem

ruling out
alternatives

for a purpose

the torus
this is astrophysics
actually
not a new experience

an orgy for two
a smorgasbord for the One World
cornucopia as the shape of the space-time
    continuum

explanations for energy leaks

an anomaly
for and against generative constancy
a paradox
in search of

explications
against mistakes
for deliberate misinterpretation
endless projections of insularity
conceit
ego
can't get it out of the mind
as if the only inside-out were
getting turned out
were inversion

nevermind

no mind
Zen, but with Western proof
then it's the depths
of shapes
diagrammatic
inner space and outer space
meditation
mediation
3D geometries
of diaphragmatic breathing

the cyclone
force effects of Earth's magnetic poles
beyond the atmosphere
otherwise known as the magnetosphere
two in love and lovemaking

one in brain and mind
the multitude of Babel in temporality

the torus,
an o, doughnut, thick ring
wave form rotated on its axis
dynamics in balance
the curving of inside to outside
and back again
three-way spin: up-down, in-out, across
nonstop turning organizing complexity
warping volumes
energy churning—generating?—continuously
akin to the surface of a Moebius strip
but even so
even that a doughnut with a twist,
the torus

sense in its extension
like the eye inclusive of its sight
vision
the I in eternity
eating its existence
chewing the truth

peripherals
privilege

for all animals
ingesters
from mouth to anus
represent

that same shape

the gesture of the vortex
the jester of the cyclone
the geometry of the cosmos

for there are precise schematics
no need to speak of
the mystic interlock of outside and in
or Biblical proportions of part-to-whole
the organism imagined as and in its toroidal field
and known as a doughnut
long narrow hole
all through throat and intestines
(when Einstein claimed imagination was more important than knowledge he wasn't talking about flower fairylands and rainbow puppies, but geometric visualizations, imaginary numbers, mathematical loops and flux, hypercubes and multidimensionality, cosmic curvature, and tori; okay, he was talking about play for sure, and maybe flower fairylands and rainbow puppies too. This is a fun funnel)
pulled from inner circumference outward
graphic
almost like a cartoon
so that the whole universe is inside the organism
and with an edge scarlet as tissue lining
all its organs—kidneys, liver, heart, and associated
branching dripping pipework—stretch across the
   sky,
galactic clusters

now that's sick
and this is science

and everyone has
his or her

kinks

or should

like his and her
towels on
the towel rack
in an upstairs bathroom

at least
if there's a leak
in the wall
you'll know it

Stay Free

Timbre,
microdroplets.

People do communicate.

Dear Achiever,
      A single word can change your life. Do you want to make more money? Do you want to be an effective leader, with influence over large numbers of people? Attention everyone, the knish man is on the premises.

The gypsum shade, and sheave at diorama or even diorama as in escape. Leach. Leach it white. Oh, how dear you are to me! Pearl replied. We met when we were in school. People do communicate —it isn't in the words, terms are convoluted, definitions need definitions, too much sliding. All the arguments against meaning in words, how they weave social fabrics with oppressive fibers, how language frames realities falsely, how dominant power controls the terms. We never took no shit from no one, we weren't fools. I'm thinking of trading in my old Volkswagen. I'm thinking of trading in soybeans.

And yet, people do communicate, it isn't in the words, but they do get it, meaning gets understood between people, it happens all the time. Sometimes between only two people, intimately, one-on-one. Don't do it, Pearl! I could have held him around the neck and cried true. What a delightful and indestructible entertainment, Biggs. Backsliding, smoking menthols. I'm remembering reading Huang Po's *On the Transmission of Mind*. Oy vay.

Dollops, preposterous, I door you.

My stanched pledge and no heart. Silk flu mask offers new effective comfortable protection. That well-remembered style of face turned up. Now suddenly lifting her eyes up to mine and speaking in a different manner.

All hazards on sick leave. That upturned face, that style of face upturned. Silken flu mask. Claims of your own family I believe unless I had asked. Have a weal cutlet, eye ascent. I might sleep again perhaps in my old room.

 A reporter once asked Arnold Schwarzenegger how he was able to reach the top in body-building and as a Hollywood actor. Without hesitating, Schwarzenegger replied, "DRIVE!" That was all he said. Jaded and haggard with determination, try billionth pleat. Who had got the fidgets in his legs. Be there again soon no doubt, and putting them through all kinds of contortions in his small pantry.

This was due to the remarkable filtering properties of the silk, which causes droplets and particles to adhere to the crossweave fabric. Wasn't inhale voluntarism, such harsh influenza-ridden conditions.

Afterwards confined.

She had too, I must have shown as much on my face for her eyes were in a moment cast dowse.

Afterwards conflicted.

invest yourself, and him, and your family with

the Tao, the Dow Jones
no doubts

a golden halo, a protective, nurturing, celebratory aura of

I don't know, the bone replied. I didn't make the world. A golf term, an order for one's chauffeur, a sexual innuendo. Laden dispute funnel for turnkey. Piss on everyone. An immense fourpost somber in it which was quite a little landed disparate. See infrared maul. When we got thrown out I left without much fuss.

Douse. That diplomat's subtlety, that practice of "a word to the wise" worldliness, code words perhaps of class and insider belonging in whatever social, business, cultural, or subculture-whacked context. In the yes, in the know. And but for the promptitude of the devoted, an attunement, and understanding that the sophisticate has. Sophisticated in what? In whatever one wants to get into. I might sleep again perhaps. No doubt I might sleep again.

      In fact, throughout history, the people with the most DRIVE have accomplished the most, earned the most money and respect, had the most luck, and garnered the most power. The impending shadow of a great affliction and great disgrace that had no distinct form as yet. Felt as if the tinkers blackened and had been the better for it. From which I infer that poisoning is not always   Jeep   Hummer coronary
            was at Arlington when that happened plenum
                  afloat at bullwhip or even digging as indignant
                                    puddles under the grave.

A free feeling. A song by the Clash that always gives me that feeling—of nostalgia, of lost youth, of lost wildness. Of stirring youth, of stirring wildness. The Jam, v-neck shirts and baggy trousers. Not smoking menthols. Smoking cloves, at Santa Monica beach in ninth grade, station nine, the "Valley" station, I was astray. I'm only just beginning to live, Pearl whispered back. I don't want it to end. What the hell is going on, Pearl? I went to Woodstock.

Its middle layer an organic membrane that comes from the Mulberry Tree. Wouldn't every good invention be? It was his spirit not his constitution. The patrimony ill-served him. With widespread use, a contributor to lessening a major global threat. Wouldn't every good intention be?

"You've got to want it."

On total resignation, not to be obtained. Over the beard sign fire, approval-manager. You're shtupping the blouse man, aren't you? It'd be crazy to have your mother-in-law know.

My blue hearsay but I shall confide in you just the same, Carmelina. There are different kinds of pearls, as there are different Pearls in question. Not just the same Pearl. Just the same Carmelina. There's a Pearl played by Diane Lane, and there's a Pearl who's a sweet pig in an illustrated children's book.

birth of the son, the daughter starting school

    faces upturned   by the light of your
                                                                    countenance

the baby's punim as if translucent from a source just beneath the skin, or reflecting bone-deep off the facial structure a source from above, from the spiritual beyond. Not concise, not merely the precise word, more than a word to the. Not so ambassadorial, that, not tact, but governmental to be sure, lots of garrulousness ala Alan Greenspan. See grammarian Georgeta. Oracular pronouncements as well, argot. Our gut feeling that. There only some words count, only some phrases are clues, and those in the know clue in. The initiated hear it when it sounds, or the instinctive grasper, naturally. There's a greed for worldly wisdom and gain, both, providential for prosperity, and with it a tendency to go on and on. Up and up. Plus, divine hints. It's all on the up-and-up. I'm thinking of trading in emissions credits. I'm thinking of trading in.

Applies too to every profession, every specialty, specialization, and quackery, anything concomitant with the diction of advanced degrees, and no less to the academic avant-garde in arts and writing. Embedded in it, the few keys. Either towards higher understanding, or petty getting ahead. Divine hints are a plus, but only if one is adding up to greatness. Ingots in the argot;

otherwise, stick to the letter of your jargon—cant, for those who can't. There is glory in art, there is glory in love, there is glory in writing. Deny it, if you dare, and relegate yourself to mediocrity. Dismiss, disdain. Out of hatred of the shiny, you may have your momentary revenge, but you've become a self-selected dud. Dullard.

Can I ask you one question? Did I want a microscope? When you lot get out we're gonna hit the town, we'll burn it fuckin' down—to a cinder. Hurry, these offers expire TONIGHT! The stated, a cheerful incursion. He asked me what I take with it, and proffered a few ripe teaches, some whole, some sliced. I was a stray. The ice cream man is on the premises. Reconsider, reestablish the premises. Pith o' sense and pride o' worth. That style of face turned up. Turned up faces, upturned faces; eyes upward, uprolling eyes. Cosmically-intoxicated! Wait, it's just the everyday. I practiced daily in my room. Disagreeable in some stages of the process. Of the progress. Bone, say something to comfort me. You are very dear to me, said the bone. Get your toochis up here, Marty, I don't care whatcha gotta do. Timber!

Suppose you were to go down into the old part of the country again for instance. Supposing you were to go down. We went to the pose airflow at conspirator diacritic then. Being in a beastly condition and our hoist heated enough. Manya the lion. née Manya DeLeon, Manya Magnus. We took our candles and went upstairs.

Feverish, delirious. The communication is in the moment. There will be time, there will be timbre. Communication relevant to the context in the present, and absolute only in and for the time being, in that a matter of timeliness. Timeliness and transcendence. A word's definition isn't for all time, but each person knows, can know, what each is talking about for that time. You give me fever. We're talking accomplished communication, involving listening, and attunement, and when that works it works beyond the words. Same goes for morality and forms—absolutes are elsewhere, principles can be eternal, but laws and commands and formulations can't be. They are produced in time, not relative, absolutes are everywhere, but manifested differently according to the times. It isn't an absolute Thou Shalt Not Kill, and there're all sorts of configurations when it comes to universal love, the immoral included. When it comes to specifics.

The Elfic D'oracle   speaking
and specifying   signaling, and signifying
of the Barbarous Names of Evocation
and towards the Transmission of Mind.

She can be reached. Manya Magnus Earthlingk. I can be reached, we can be reached. Filtration not dependent solely on pore size @conspirator-diacritic.com. Not breached, but reached. Electrostatic properties of silk.

M., and magma.

My magma, I'm magma

magma   magmagnus@earthlink.net
magma(gnus) @ magma agnus @ earthling.net
                              earthlink/ earthling/ earthlingk
                              go easy/ step lightly/ stay free

Mag-Mag, Inc.
Magma Ink

hear the gnus
Hero Magnus, daughter   Gryphon Magnus, son
Gryphon Magnus' Hebrew name: Shmuel Harel
            ben Malka Leah ben Magus Avraham

By way of a name. Mallymoo, and Beakyberker Land, which has to be extremely cold. Three years in Brixton. Was a little concert that she'd lose her place on the page, and so reminded her to read with her index. Then there was Incheletta, Inchie for short, a proper name for her little finger, commonly known as the pinky. By way of a word.

That understood word as the medium, as the point of focus if nothing else, the contact. By way of a word much gets transferred—much subliminal meaning, much psychic meaning, thought transference. Two people, or more, do understand each other when they speak, a person can indeed read and understand. Insistence, that trying climate the intuitions. Poor qualitative Jack. What I have endured and do endure here is insupportable.

Chemistry, magnetism, yin and yang, insight,
        inflow, yin flow, pussy power.
               Cock power.

And these teaches   new teaches, blue teaches   one fish, tuna fish
        The Teaches of Peaches

Evangeline's vagina, by way of a name.

To look watchfully at her for suggestions.
  Choices, choices. *The Blessing of a Skinned Knee: using Jewish teachings to raise self-reliant children* tonight, or
        Abel Ferrara's *Nine Lives of a Wet Pussy*?

You're an amazing bone, said Pearl, and this is a day I won't ever forget!

 Since you're reading this letter, I believe you already have more DRIVE than most of the population. Most people would have carelessly tossed this letter aside. But you're reading because you're smarter than they are—and more driven to succeed. I'm thinking of trading in futures. I'm thinking of trading in my legs for motorized pogo sticks.

Dario Fo's "infant prattle" and Robert Burns' "bickerin' brattle." Wee, sleekit, cowrin', tim'rous beastie. Not my strong daughter, Hero Magnus, first girl on

Mars. Or what she wills, or what the voice inside her calls her for. Meanwhile, she calls out. My hair is socking wet. Sleepovers are a big lump of fun. You know those ugly black squirrels around here? Well, a few weeks ago, Mom and I saw one black squirrel that was as beautiful as a flying lion.

Therefore Nietzsche, from *Philosophy in the Tragic Age of the Greeks*: "…will also rejoice in philosophical systems, even if completely erroneous. They always have one wholly incontrovertible point: personal mood, color."
    one holy incontrovertible point.
    a man's a man for a' that.
    and a woman as well or more, a person, an earthling

Jewish blessing before the exceptionally beautiful: "Blessed art thou, oh Lord our God, who has such in His universe."

There will be timing. I'm investing in futures. Knowing plans gang aft agley. But living with it, believing. Seeing. Surrounding Gryphon's birth, a golden halo, a protective, nurturing, celebratory aura of divinity and destiny: our charmed family, Hero's destiny, Gryphon's destiny—the daughter starting school, the birth of the son.
    By the grace of God, with gratitude to God.

Enchantress from the Stars. Or, *Seven Ravens*. In the Brothers Grimm story, a little sister who would save her seven brothers trapped in a glass mountain lost her star gift of a chicken bone, which she kept wrapped in a napkin and which was supposed to open her brothers' prison. Instead she cut off her finger, and used her own skinny bone as a key to the glass mountain. Ever must we leach the teaches, and for our daily wages waging, War of the Words, "Patristic Logomachies," A. Crowley. Suck marrow, leech. On bone-white, leech-black.

For admittedly, one can signal discreetly all one's life, with sophistication and subtlety, also no doubt losing it, in fits of desperation waving frantically, flagrantly. No matter, if no one's there to match it. Outside of one's inner circle, outside of love's invented language. He asked me what I take with it.

Not failed to make upon society lured me away. Birds is got weary shy. No matter, if no one's there with willingness or understanding or attunement or the least receptivity, no one outside, no object of the preposition from the word to, no objectivity as to the absolute import of the subjective, no one to take the word in its transmission. In its transference, as in psychoanalytic love, but is there really any love for the analyst? No wise ones in, in no wise. If no one gets it, it isn't really sufficient. So what is sufficient and beyond the words? Self-sufficiency?

Brecht in Santa Monica (1941-1947)

Marcuse at UCSD (1965-1970)

Antaeus / Anchises

The Giant of Greek myth was an invincible wrestler because when he touched the Earth, his mother, his strength was renewed. Hercules killed him by holding him aloft and throttling him.

At the fall of Troy, in an act millennially-famous for its filial piety, Aeneas carried his father to safety on his shoulders. It is said the fires gave way to make a path for them.

The Giant's father was the sea, Poseidon, and his mother the Earth, Gaea. The old man was beloved of Aphrodite as a youth, and they gave birth to the destined Father of Rome, a fled son of destroyed Troy.

At the birth of my son I am long estranged from my father, and I hear he's seriously ailing. I hate him for this, and for more than this.

Birdman in a No-Fly Zone

urgencies needed   or ascribed
     lessened the cause for   percolations
busted lungs   divulged   alveoli ravioli

gurgling, the last breath   the last word seals it
      "I've got my ass on the moon, I'm shaking my butt
    on the moon!" said Neil Armstrong,
                        after a step.

the bubbles, the coffee grounds
                   it's busted, it's blood

post-step

new procedures for reshapening the heart
                          its blood
                  carvings
of the fat-marbled   the hardened   ricotta
terra cotta   it's cheap, saving your life
besides insurance will cover it
                    and the tax-payers

twisted niggardliness of spirit   intimacy just a little
     smiles, manipulation   trust me
       a Pyrex coffeepot makes a great   defense
weapon   if you swing it the right way
                     full and hot

faces melted   like the wings of Icarus
         No, not at all like that,
    you classical bastard.

It just feels like that because of clogged sinuses,
                                take a pseudophed.

a bacillus is a rod-shaped bacteria
        a basilisk blinds you with a look
                rather, kills you with a look.
I've some sneaking suspicions that science
would have something to say
                about this
but my own physiology prevents me from following up on the ideal
                                        with my family practitioner.

take a spray

can't you get some of that from bananas?   kidney function
phosphorescent levels in the blood   He failed a potassium test,
and now we're worried about closure.   And politicization,
Cheney doesn't need to be brought into this even with his defibrillator.

little bubbles, little bursts of light
                                it hasn't stopped any fibbing
carry the O_2 on a red disk-shaped cell
                      and then there're the green globes
hemoglobin   pyrotechnics
                glow balls, a slight cast to the clear spheres
                                    of green
                        bubbles—the perfect tension.

paved intentions   you know how you'll end up
        choking on your own   justified means
                                        eating the children

until you can't breath anymore for emphysema and toadying
                                      the thin air up there

is it heart failure or failure of the heart?
that's a sentimental question, and I diagnose   art disease
         Prognosis: not good.

lessen the iridescence   the wax, like butter
   like garlic bread   sop up the meat sauce
         entrails of a contrail flyer

seppuku   reveal you my innards, warrior
     "Through death, I shall not lose my honor.
     Here I am. I show you, here I am."
         or, more American and clinging to the vain,
     "You think you know me? Do you think you know me?!"
                divulge you, divulge you.

the vein, the vine

come to the table for dinner
we all eat together as a family
     Don't you fuckin' touch that axe!
that's mine, and mine alone.
         the patriarch, the fasces.

did I hear some asshole academic   some *critic*
talking about a "minor" aesthetics
         poetry of the mundane,
                inanity
this is a horror genre   and domesticity is hell
and you shouldn't get close to anyone for fear of the devil inside
     gaping maws of infernos   and stomach cancers
    bleeding ulcers   intestinal convolutions
the truth

urgencies ascribed   and needed

      a cause for the popping of bubbles, a gurgling
busted breath   and now an operation on the vocal chords
     but I'm not gonna say anything at your funeral

this relationship has expired
this intention has expired
this ideology has expired
this democracy has expired
your parental authority has expired
this aesthetic has expired
this false claim, this lie   has expired
     and you're expiring, and you think that means
                           all bets are off.

but I'm invested elsewhere
                 I've put my money
                          on something else
my ones
                my ones and onlys
                        (there *are* a few!)
                  and my lonely arson,
                      my lonely asking.
my hedgehopping, but no hedging.

Freedom in the real, only in the real.
        Mortality brings you back to it   or not

The choice is either toadying or True Love.

Thole Econometrica, Thole Apocalypse

Are you ignoring me? debilitate
on satisfactory be bloodwrought its convolution the
    phoneme!
to kiss her fan again to shake it and the anaplasmosis
    who was looking at us in a state of
to waive it
how the patricians girl or mendacity. Advantage!
sand it forklift nor gauge nor desist archfool and
    citation
Appian, anew
Rome may derail the bold
bald electorate lackadaisical and tooth
forsooth the anaglyph
in ramrod a switch may
I must have shown as much in my face for her eyes
    were in a moment downcast and I saw tears in
                                  them

the holeable or plutonium some desultory it
thole able, syllables, syllabub
emotion on elevate, madden
opus or bravery but circulate
battlefield it's brinksmanship it's
curriculum—hey Bub, counteract on increasables!

bliss
lolly may
amalgam the crush
cupid gynocentric mush on tramway

an invitation I was only too proud and happy to
    accept
dynamics persist the mingled reality
curvilinear it caught some ascension!
gyroscope! summertime a coincident utopia, try
                                          snafu

the horsemen counting by ampere hours
Cinerama its blister sum dictate the pageant it's
lens be leitmotif devolve on infinitum, add on
she seemed to avoid his look with such unwonted
    hesitation and timidity
deuce it congeals in stratospheric torpor
hemorrhage attrition and pessimism some ecstasy
dozens some otherworldly my semaphore
watch but abstract!
abreact
but substantiate its buttress to the exterior
blood rot
be expedient
frizzle its interim with blueprint try sane
it's the same ellipsis doctrine
not anthem be tart
page congrats
abraxas

anonymous, Antaeus, show appetite is lunatic
stick tight Byzantium and give it its brick
some needlework and diffracted signals
continuity and nut or rivet and downdraft
then I saw as though all the intervening time had

    been canceled and I was still standing
someone of a nobler character shall have nothing to
    think of then
            implied the predisposition with a smile
a chariot together banish its aerosol
were so dazzling and opened up such illimitable
    regions of delight
where I had sat in the sun and in the shade waiting
    for my money
invidious be labile
being able to keep back and make a clumsy laugh of
                                            it

gild and anonymity labia a factorial babysit
I assented to this proposal in default of being able
where I worked and played as a boy and did it a
    cruel wrong
the cupidity not conciliatory whichever cyclorama
on its swivel
switched-over
annunciate some broth some breadth some utility
add-ons with nightfall afforestation aghast
that out of the way woman with the savagest of
    names
passed the veritable
and the sense of being unfit for it or of not having
    understood it or of having shown
embellished over the dazzle shopworn fire
to return with a meaning it had never had before
plebe bargain

suspicions arose within her that it was an
    ill-assorted friendship

a consortium of diffraction factoids, singleds
I'd observed a gradual alteration and had often
   wondered whether she had too

she had to
would be dragged at the heels of any number of
                                   wild horses,
       why should she confine herself to four?
I had to, desultory suspicions arose within me
lessons
               why should she confide herself?
the holeable, the phony throng of fusion, fission
my semaphore
pageant the aerosol, its arsenal—torched!
a chariot switched o'er

the latter point I achieved at great personal
                             inconvenience

Vermifuge

where contempt finds its path to you
the worm
vermillion

longitudinal fortitude
intestines' intricacies
asking for latitude
longing for

shadow feeling
phantom limb

a limping intimation

that segment of
verisimilitude

has you squirmy
for the labyrinth

has you at
a dead end

which way the arrow on its pivot

muscling of the beat
the fort of the chest
your spectral core
torso's organ double

ka of *coeur fort*

has you squishy
for dignity
for finding the thread

but what to go for
center

or
exit

Anthem / Anathema

Magus Magnus lives and writes
in Alexandria, Virginia.